My Baby
Record Book

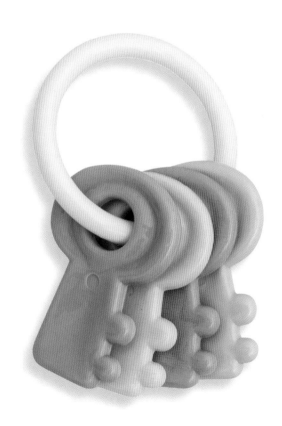

Published by Hinkler Books Pty Ltd
45–55 Fairchild Street
Heatherton Victoria 3202 Australia
www.hinkler.com.au

hinkler

Text © Hinkler Books Pty Ltd 2004, 2010, 2011
Design © Hinkler Books Pty Ltd 2010, 2011
This edition published 2013 for Index Books Ltd.

Author: Kate Cody
Cover design: Hinkler Books Studio
Design: Sonia Dixon
Prepress: Graphic Print Group

ISBN: 978 1 7418 3776 6

Printed and bound in China

My Baby

Record Book

Your Baby's Birth

Name

....

Date of birth

....

Place of birth

....

....

....

Day of the week

....

Time of birth

....

Birth weight

....

Birth length

....

Head circumference

....

Delivered by

....

Name of doctor

....

Name of midwife

....

About the birth

....

....

....

....

....

Baby looks like

....

....

....

....

Baby's eyes are

....

Baby's hair is

....

Baby's star sign

....

One for luck, two for joy,
Three for a girl, four for a boy.

Visitors

....

....

....

....

....

....

....

Cards, flowers and presents

....

....

....

....

....

....

Memorable moments

....

....

....

....

....

Baby's birth photo

Early Days at Home

Sleeping Routine

Visitors

....

....

....

....

Cards, flowers and presents

....

....

....

....

....

Memorable moments

....

....

....

....

....

Sleeping times

....

....

Waking times

....

....

....

Feeding Routine

Duration of feed

....

Description of feed

....

....

....

Newspaper birth announcement

Memorable moments

....

....

....

Welcome to the World

Our country's leader

....

News headlines

....

....

Cost of a loaf of bread

....

Cost of a stamp

....

Cost of a newspaper

....

Memorable moments

....

....

....

Birth announcement card

Higgledy piggledy my little hen,
She lays eggs for gentlemen.
Sometimes nine and sometimes ten,
Higgledy piggledy my little hen.

Naming Your Baby

Baby's name

....

....

Reason for choosing name

....

....

Other names considered

....

....

....

Nicknames

....

....

Naming Ceremony

Date

....

Place

....

Baby's outfit

....

....

Godparents

....

....

....

Naming day photo

Description of naming ceremony
and celebration

Cards and presents

How baby behaved

....

....

....

....

....

....

Who was there

....

....

....

....

....

....

....

....

....

....

....

Two little dickey-birds
sitting on a wall,
One named Peter,
One named Paul.
Fly away Peter,
Fly away Paul.
Come back Peter!
Come back Paul!

Baby's Family Tree

Your Baby's Family

Mother's birth date

....

Mother's place of birth

....

....

Mother's life story in a nutshell

....

....

....

....

....

....

....

....

....

Father's birth date

....

Father's place of birth

....

....

Father's life story in a nutshell

....

....

....

....

....

....

....

....

....

Significant family dates

....

....

....

....

Brothers and sisters

....

....

....

Ages of brothers and sisters

....

....

....

great grandmother	great grandfather	great grandmother	great grandfather	great grandmother	great grandfather	great grandmother	great grandfather
....	....	....	....	....	....	....	....
....	....	....	....	....	....	....	....

grandmother

grandfather

grandmother

grandfather

....

mother

father

....

baby

....

Sleepy Nights

Description of baby's nursery

....

....

....

Description of the cot/crib

....

....

....

First slept in cot/crib

....

....

First slept in own room

....

....

First slept through the night

....

....

Memorable moments

....

....

Little Boy Blue

Come blow your horn,

The sheep's in the meadow

The cow's in the corn.

Where is the boy

Who looks after the sheep?

He's under the haystack

Fast asleep!

12

Helping Your Baby to Sleep

Going to bed routine at night

....

....

....

Lullabies that baby loves

....

....

....

Bedtime stories that baby loves

....

....

Bedtime toys or comforters

....

....

Settling techniques tried

....

....

Baby asleep

Most successful settling technique

....

....

....

....

....

....

Food to Grow

Food and Drink Firsts

First began eating puréed food

....
....

First began eating mashed food

....
....

First began eating solid food

....

Foods that baby loves

....

First drank from a spout cup

....

First drank through a straw

....

First drank from a cup

....

First sat in a high chair

....
....

First ate with a spoon

....

First began sharing the family meal

....

Known food sensitivities

....
....

Memorable moments

....
....
....

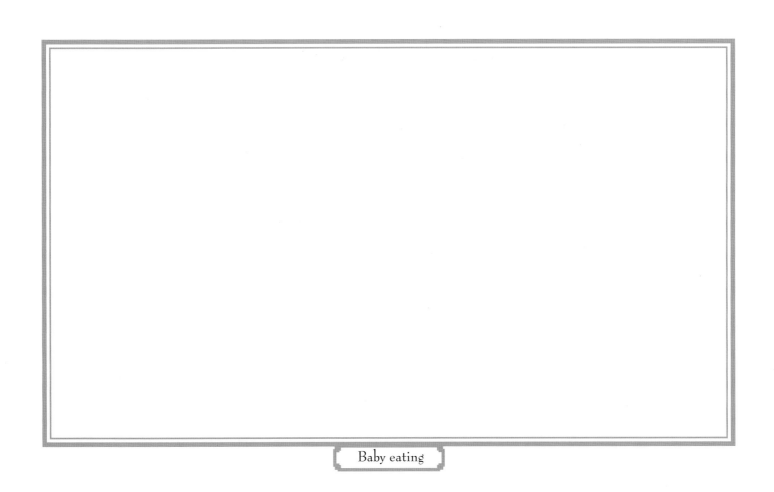

Baby eating

Pat a cake, pat a cake, baker's man,
Bake me a cake as fast as you can.
Pat it and prick it and mark it with B,
And put it in the oven for baby and me.

Developmental Milestones

Began following with eyes

....

....

Began turning head to sound

....

....

First smiled

....

....

Began grasping rattle or soft toy

....

....

Began putting rattle or toy to mouth

....

....

First cooed

....

....

First held up head

....

....

First rolled over

....

....

Growing baby

Began to sit alone

....

....

First crawled

....

....

First stands with support

....

....

Began to walk with support

....

....

Started babbling

....

....

First words

....

....

....

Started taking steps

....

....

Walked alone

....

....

....

First tooth

....

....

Sally go round the sun,
Sally go round the moon,
Sally go round the chimney pots,
On a Sunday afternoon.

Things Baby Loves

Comforter

....

....

....

....

Things around home

....

....

....

....

Soft toys

....

....

....

Toys

....

Books

....

....

....

Nursery rhymes

....

....

....

....

Lullabies

....

....

....

....

Animals or pets

....

....

....

Games

....

....

....

Activities

....

....

....

....

....

....

People

....

....

....

....

....

....

Places

....

....

....

....

....

....

This is the way the ladies ride,
Nimble, nimble, nimble, nimble;
This is the way the gentlemen ride,
A gallop, a trot, a gallop, a trot;
This is the way the farmers ride,
Jiggety-jog, jiggety-jog;
This is the way the farmboys ride,
Hobbledy-hoy, hobbledy-hoy;
This is the way the huntsmen ride,
A gallop, a gallop,
And down in the ditch!

Fun with Water

Bath-time

First bath

....

First time in a big bath

....

Began sharing a bath

....

....

Bath toys

....

....

Bath games

....

....

Water Play

First trip to the beach or lake

....

First water play in garden

....

....

Rub-a-dub dub,

Three men in a tub,

And who do you think they be?

A butcher, a baker,

A candle-stick maker,

Turn them out,

Knaves all three!

First splash in paddling pool

....

....

First dip in swimming pool

....

....

First swimming class

....

....

....

....

Your baby's swimming costume

....

....

....

....

....

You shall have a fishy
On a little dishy,
You shall have a fishy
When the boat comes in.

Baby in the bath

Going Out

First playgroup

....
....
....

First time baby fed the ducks

....
....

First visit to the playground

....
....
....

First time on a merry-go-round

....
....
....

First visit to the zoo

....
....
....

Family weekend activities

....
....
....

Going Out to:

The swimming pool

....
....
....

Cafes and restaurants

....
....
....

The shops

....
....
....
....

Parks and gardens

....
....
....

The beach

....
....
....

The countryside

....
....
....

Bus

....

....

....

....

Visiting
Grandparents

....

....

....

Relatives

....

....

....

Friends

....

....

....

Trips by:
Pram/stroller

....

....

....

....

Car

....

....

....

Train

....

....

....

Plane

....

....

Other

....

....

....

Clever Baby

First waved goodbye

....

....

First played peek-a-boo

....

....

First clapped hands

....

....

First pulled a pull-along toy

....

....

First picked up tiny objects

....

....

First stacked blocks

....

....

First turned the pages of a book

....

....

First joined in singing a song

....

....

First put on their own clothes

....

....

First danced

....

....

Other baby firsts

....

....

....

....

....

....

....

....

....

....

....

One, two,
Buckle my shoe.
Three, four,
Knock on the door.
Five, six,
Pick up sticks.
Seven, eight,
Lay them straight.
Nine, ten,
Big fat hen!

Clever baby

Round and round the garden,
Like a teddy bear.
One step, two steps,
Tickle you under there!

Healthy Baby

Vaccinations

Age	Vaccinations	Date Given*
Birth	Hepatitis B	
2 months	Diptheria/Tetanus/Pertussis Oral Polio Vaccine Hepatitis B H. Influenzae Type b	
4 months	Diptheria/Tetanus/Pertussis Oral Polio Vaccine Hepatitis B H. Influenzae Type b	
6 months	Diptheria/Tetanus/Pertussis Oral Polio Vaccine	
12 months	Measles/Mumps/Rubella Hepatitis B H. Influenzae Type b	

Other Vaccinations

Age	Vaccinations	Date Given

Any reactions

....

....

....

....

....

....

Note – vaccination schedules may vary. The above is a guide only.

Health and
Development Checks
Health care professionals

....
....
....
....
....
....

Visits to health care professionals

Age	Date	Comment

Three cheeky monkeys,

Bouncing on the bed,

One fell off and bumped his head.

Mama called the doctor,

And the doctor said;

No more monkeys,

Bouncing on the bed!

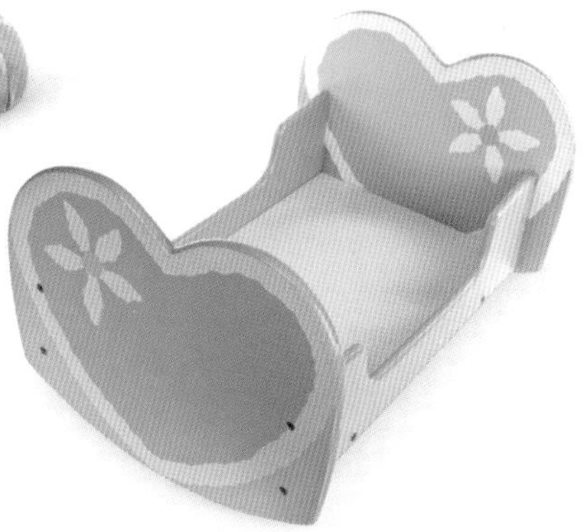

2 Months Old

Usually woke for the day at

....

Went to bed for the day at

....

Daytime sleep routine

....

....

....

....

Daytime feeding routine

....

....

....

Night-time sleeping
and feeding routine

....

....

....

Weight

....

Length

....

Head circumference

....

Crying periods

....

....

....

....

Best way to calm your baby

....

....

....

....

....

Changes

....

....

....

....

New sounds

....

....

....

....

....

New firsts

....

....

....

....

....

Your baby's temperament

....

....

....

....

Nicknames

....

....

....

....

Description of a typical day

....

....

....

....

Baby at 2 months

Photo caption

....

....

....

Date photo taken

....

....

4 Months Old

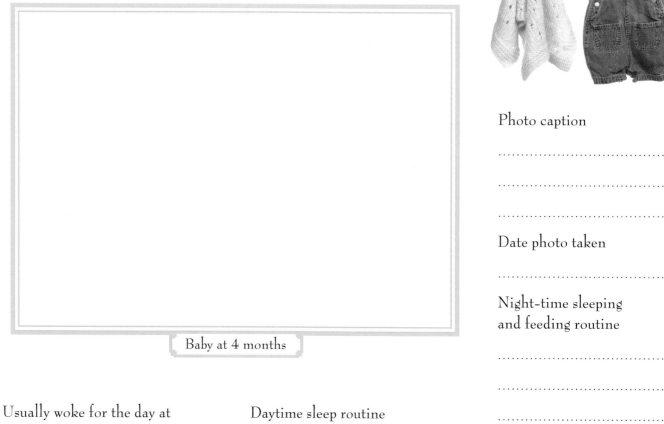

Baby at 4 months

Photo caption

....

....

....

Date photo taken

....

Night-time sleeping
and feeding routine

....

....

....

Weight

....

Length

....

Head circumference

....

Usually woke for the day at

....

....

Went to bed for the day at

....

....

Daytime sleep routine

....

....

Daytime feeding routine

....

....

30

Time spent playing on the floor

....

....

....

....

Crying periods

....

....

....

Best way to calm your baby

....

....

....

....

Changes

....

....

....

New sounds

....

....

....

New firsts

....

....

....

....

Your baby's temperament

....

....

....

Nicknames

....

....

....

Description of a typical day

....

....

....

Preferred activities

....

....

Preferred foods

....

....

....

....

....

....

....

6 Months Old

Usually woke for the day at

....

Went to bed for the day at

....

....

Daytime sleep routine

....

....

Daytime feeding routine

....

....

Night-time sleeping
and feeding routine

....

....

....

....

Weight

....

Length

....

Head circumference

....

Time spent playing on the floor

....

....

Crying periods

....

....

....

Best way to calm your baby

....

....

....

....

Changes

....

....

....

New teeth

....

....

Teething symptoms and remedies

....

....

....

....

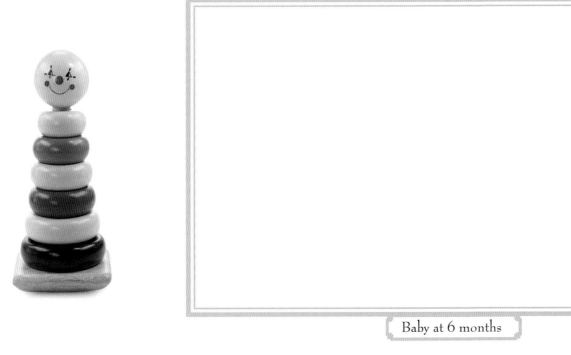

Baby at 6 months

New sounds

....

....

New firsts

....

....

....

Your baby's temperament

....

....

....

Nicknames

....

....

Description of a typical day

....

....

Preferred activities

....

....

....

Photo caption

....

....

....

Date photo taken

....

Preferred foods

....

....

....

8 Months Old

Usually woke for the day at

....

....

Went to bed for the day at

....

....

Daytime sleep routine

....

....

Daytime feeding routine

....

....

Night-time sleeping
and feeding routine

....

....

....

Photo caption

....

....

....

....

Date photo taken

....

....

Baby at 8 months

Weight

....

Length

....

Head circumference

....

Time spent playing on the floor

....

....

Crying periods

....

....

....

Best way to calm your baby

....

....

....

Changes

....

....

....

New teeth

....

....

....

Teething symptoms and remedies

....

....

....

New sounds

....

New firsts

....

....

Your baby's temperament

....

....

Nicknames

....

Description of a typical day

....

....

....

Preferred activities

....

....

....

Preferred foods

....

....

10 Months Old

Usually woke for the day at

....

Went to bed for the day at

....

Daytime sleep routine

....

....

Daytime feeding routine

....

....

Night-time sleeping
and feeding routine

....

....

....

Weight

....

Length

....

Head circumference

....

Time spent playing on the floor

....

....

Crying periods

....

....

....

Best way to calm your baby

....

....

....

Changes

....

....

New teeth

....

....

Teething symptoms and remedies

....

....

....

Baby at 10 months

New sounds

....

....

New firsts

....

....

....

....

Your baby's temperament

....

....

Nicknames

....

....

Description of a typical day

....

....

....

Preferred activities

....

....

....

Photo caption

....

....

....

Date photo taken

....

Preferred foods

....

....

....

12 Months Old

Usually woke for the day at

....

....

Went to bed for the day at

....

....

Daytime sleep routine

....

....

Daytime feeding routine

....

....

Night-time sleeping
and feeding routine

....

....

....

Photo caption

....

....

....

....

Date photo taken

....

....

Baby at 12 months

Weight

....

Length

....

Head circumference

....

Time spent playing on the floor

....

....

Crying periods

....

....

Best way to calm your baby

....

....

....

Changes

....

....

New teeth

....

....

....

Teething symptoms and remedies

....

....

....

New sounds

....

New firsts

....

Your baby's temperament

....

Nicknames

....

Description of a typical day

....

....

....

Preferred activities

....

....

....

Preferred foods

....

....

....

Your Baby's Firsts

First smile

....

....

First gripped rattle

....

....

First laughed

....

....

First tooth

....

....

First haircut

....

....

Clever baby

First slept through the night

....

....

First said 'Mama'

....

....

....

Photo caption

....

....

....

....

Date photo taken

....

First said 'Dada'

....

....

First waved goodbye

....

....

First rolled

....

....

First sat

....

....

First crawled

....

....

First stood

....

....

First walked

....

....

First babysitter

....

....

I had a little nut tree,
Nothing would it bear,
But a silver nutmeg,
And a golden pear.

First Christmas

Christmas Eve
Where the day was spent

....
....
....
....
....

Who was there

....
....
....
....

Baby's outfit

....
....

Description of your baby's
first Christmas Eve

....
....
....

Christmas Day
Where the day was spent

....
....
....
....
....

Who was there

....
....
....
....

Your present to your baby

....
....
....
....
....

Other presents

....
....
....
....

Present your baby loved the most

....

....

First Christmas meal

....

....

....

Baby's outfit

....

....

Description of the Christmas tree

....

....

....

Description of your baby's first
Christmas Day

....

....

....

....

*On the first day of Christmas
My true love gave to me
A partridge in a pear tree.*

First Christmas

Photo caption

....

....

Date photo taken

....

....

First Birthday

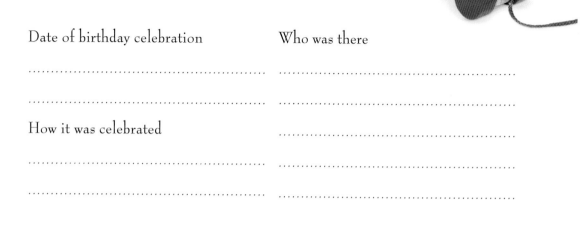

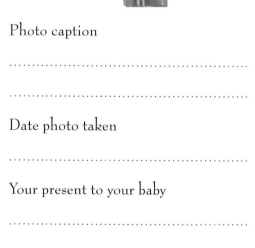

Date of birthday celebration

....

....

How it was celebrated

....

....

Who was there

....

....

....

....

Photo caption

....

....

Date photo taken

....

Your present to your baby

....

....

....

....

First birthday

Other presents

....

....

....

....

....

Baby's outfit

....

How baby behaved

....

....

....

Baby's reaction when
'Happy Birthday' sung

....

....

....

....

....

Description of cake

....

....

....

Description of birthday celebration

....

....

....

....

....

....

Memorable moments

....

....

....

....

....

Going on Holiday

First Holiday

People who went

....
....
....
....

How long away

....
....
....

Getting there details

....
....
....

Accommodation details

....
....
....
....

Toys and books taken

....
....
....

Baby's holiday routine

....
....
....

New experiences

....
....
....

Holiday highlights

....
....
....

Memorable moments

....
....
....
....
....

Other Holidays

Holiday highlights

....
....
....

Memorable moments

....
....
....

On holiday

Photo caption

....

....

Date photo taken

....

The grand old Duke of York,

He had ten thousand men,

He marched them up to the top of the hill,

Then he marched them down again!

And when they were up they were up,

And when they were down they were down,

And when they were only halfway up,

They were neither up nor down.

47

Looking Back

Baby's First Year

Greatest pleasure

....
....
....
....
....
....

Greatest challenge

....
....
....
....
....

Siblings' early reaction to baby

....
....
....
....
....
....

Siblings' relationship
with baby now

....
....
....
....
....
....

Your baby's personality

....
....
....
....
....
....

Thoughts on being a family

....
....
....
....
....